HONOURS LIST

LEAGUE CHAMPIONS
1900-01, 1905-06, 1921-22, 1922-23, 1946-47,
1963-64, 1965-66, 1972-73, 1975-76, 1976-77,
1978-79, 1979-80, 1981-82, 1982-83, 1983-84,
1985-86, 1987-88, 1989-90

EUROPEAN CUP / CHAMPIONS LEAGUE WINNERS
1976-77, 1977-78, 1980-81, 1983-84, 2004-05, 2018-19

FA CUP WINNERS
1964-65, 1973-74, 1985-86, 1988-89, 1991-92,
2000-01, 2005-06

LEAGUE CUP WINNERS
1980-81, 1981-82, 1982-83, 1983-84, 1994-95,
2000-01, 2002-03, 2011-12

UEFA CUP WINNERS
1972-73, 1975-76, 2000-01

UEFA SUPER CUP WINNERS
1977, 2001, 2005, 2019

FA CHARITY SHIELD WINNERS
1964*, 1965*, 1966, 1974, 1976, 1977*, 1979, 1980,
1982, 1986*, 1988, 1989, 1990*, 2001, 2006 (*shared)

FOOTBALL LEAGUE SUPER CUP WINNERS
1985-86

DIVISION TWO WINNERS
1893-94, 1895-96, 1904-05, 1961-62

LANCASHIRE LEAGUE WINNERS
1892-93

RESERVE DIVISION ONE WINNERS
1956-57, 1968-69, 1969-70, 1970-71, 1972-73,
1973-74, 1974-75, 1975-76, 1976-77, 1978-79,
1979-80, 1980-81, 1981-82, 1983-84, 1984-85,
1989-90, 1999-2000, 2007-08

FA YOUTH CUP WINNERS
1995-96, 2005-06, 2006-07, 2018-19

FA WOMEN'S SUPER LEAGUE
2013, 2014

2018/19 SEASON REVIEW

THE 2018/19 SEASON WILL FOREVER BE REMEMBERED AS ONE OF THE GREATEST IN LIVERPOOL'S HISTORY AND WITH GOOD REASON. IT WAS A CAMPAIGN IN WHICH REDS WERE CROWNED CHAMPIONS OF EUROPE FOR A SIXTH TIME AND WENT AS CLOSE AS THEY'VE EVER COME TO LANDING A FIRST PREMIER LEAGUE TITLE. FROM START TO FINISH IT WAS AN AMAZING AND EMOTIONAL ROLLER-COASTER OF A JOURNEY, ONE THAT WILL LIVE LONG IN THE MEMORY OF ALL WHO WITNESSED IT...

AUGUST

The opening month couldn't have panned out any better for Liverpool; three wins from three games, seven goals scored and none conceded, as West Ham, Crystal Palace and Brighton were all beaten. Performance-wise there was still room for improvement and tougher tests lay ahead, but the Reds were up and running, and already making their presence felt at the top end of the Premier League table.

West Ham United (h)	PL	4-0
Crystal Palace (a)	PL	2-0
Brighton & Hove Albion (h)	PL	1-0

SEPTEMBER

Elimination from the Carabao Cup at the first hurdle was disappointing but it failed to overshadow what was another excellent month for Jürgen Klopp and his team; the highlight of which was undoubtedly the back-to-back wins against Tottenham in the Premier League and PSG on matchday one of the Champions League. For the first time ever, the Reds managed to register victories in their opening seven fixtures and although Chelsea eventually put an end to that run, Daniel Sturridge's stunning late equaliser at Stamford Bridge ensured Liverpool ended September on a positive note.

Leicester City (a)	PL	2-1
Tottenham Hotspur (a)	PL	2-1
Paris Saint-Germain (h)	CL	3-2
Southampton (h)	PL	3-0
Chelsea (h)	CC	1-2
Chelsea (a)	PL	1-1

OCTOBER

Liverpool's sternest test yet came in the opening week of October. First up was a trip to Naples for a tough Champions League clash that went the way of the hosts. Then, came a visit from the reigning Premier League champions in which a tense stalemate was viewed as a point gained, especially after Riyad Mahrez spurned a late chance from the penalty spot to win the game for City. Winning ways were soon restored following the international break and by the end of the month the Reds had thankfully rediscovered their scoring touch too.

Napoli (a)	CL	0-1
Manchester City (h)	PL	0-0
Huddersfield Town (a)	PL	1-0
Red Star Belgrade (h)	CL	4-0
Cardiff City (h)	PL	4-1

NOVEMBER

While domestically all appeared well during November – with seven points from nine in the Premier League – in Europe Liverpool's form was stalling and two more away defeats threatened to derail the club's progress in the Champions League. The loss to Red Star in Serbia was a major cause for concern and, following a similar result in Paris, serious doubts about Liverpool's participation in the tournament beyond the group phase were being cast.

Arsenal (a)	PL	1-1
Red Star Belgrade (a)	CL	0-2
Fulham (h)	PL	2-0
Watford (a)	PL	3-0
Paris Saint-Germain (a)	CL	1-2

DECEMBER

It was a December to remember for Liverpool who more than rose to the gruelling challenge of eight games in four weeks to make significant progress in the two competitions they craved success in most. From Divock Origi's unforgettable late winner that secured the most dramatic of victories in the Merseyside derby, to the ease at which they defeated Manchester United and the emphatic ruthlessness of the win over Arsenal, it was a month in which the Reds just seemed to go from strength to strength and saw them reclaim top spot in the Premier League. In between, there was the small matter of a winner-takes-all clash with Napoli in the Champions League. A place in the round of 16 was the prize at stake and on a memorable night at Anfield, Mo Salah and Alisson starred at opposite ends of the pitch as the Reds secured a priceless victory.

Everton (h)	PL	1-0
Burnley (a)	PL	3-1
Bournemouth (a)	PL	4-0
Napoli (h)	CL	1-0
Manchester United (h)	PL	3-1
Wolverhampton Wanderers (a)	PL	2-0
Newcastle United (h)	PL	4-0
Arsenal (h)	PL	5-1

JANUARY

A first league defeat of the season in the much-hyped meeting of the top two at the Etihad and another domestic cup exit, this time away to Wolves in the FA Cup third round, meant it was a miserable start to the new year for Liverpool. Victories over Brighton and Crystal Palace seemingly got things back on track before a frustrating draw with Leicester at a wintry Anfield prevented the Reds from extending their advantage at the top of the Premier League table.

Manchester City (a)	PL	1-2
Wolverhampton Wanderers (a)	FA	1-2
Brighton & Hove Albion (a)	PL	1-0
Crystal Palace (h)	PL	4-3
Leicester City (h)	PL	1-1

FEBRUARY

The eagerly awaited return of Champions League football proved something of an anti-climax as Liverpool and Bayern Munich played out a cagey goalless draw in the round of 16 first leg at Anfield. Of greater concern though was the ground Manchester City were making up in the Premier League title race after the Reds dropped further points, away to West Ham and Manchester United. A 5-0 hammering of Watford on the penultimate night of the month, however, ensured they remained in pole position.

West Ham United (a)	PL	1-1
Bournemouth (h)	PL	3-0
Bayern Munich (h)	CL	0-0
Manchester United (a)	PL	0-0
Watford (h)	PL	5-0

MARCH

A goalless draw in the Merseyside derby meant the destiny of the Premier League title was no longer in Liverpool's hands but it spurred the Reds on to a phenomenal run of form. The most notable result in March came at the Allianz Arena in Munich as Jürgen Klopp celebrated his return to Germany by masterminding one of Liverpool's great European away performances. It was enough to clinch a place in the Champions League quarter-final, while nail-biting victories away to Fulham and home to Tottenham kept the Premier League dream alive.

Everton (a)	PL	0-0
Burnley (h)	PL	4-2
Bayern Munich (a)	CL	3-1
Fulham (a)	PL	2-1
Tottenham Hotspur (h)	PL	2-1

APRIL

Liverpool's relentless quest for success on two trophy fronts continued in impressive fashion throughout April. Home and away wins at the expense of Porto confirmed a comfortable passage into the last four of the Champions League. Domestically, the title race was developing into one of the most keenly contested in years and, to the annoyance of Manchester City, the Reds were refusing to buckle. Unfortunately, City were a team in form too and it was looking increasingly likely that this would be going down to the wire.

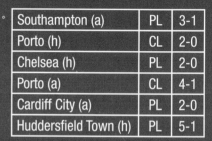

Southampton (a)	PL	3-1
Porto (h)	CL	2-0
Chelsea (h)	PL	2-0
Porto (a)	CL	4-1
Cardiff City (a)	PL	2-0
Huddersfield Town (h)	PL	5-1

MAY

A battle that had gripped the nation for almost the entire season finally reached its conclusion and despite a further two wins, it was Liverpool who were ultimately forced to concede defeat. In the end it was a heart-breaking finale for the Reds who lost just one game all campaign and finished with a club record points haul of 97. Any other season, bar three, it would have been enough to see them crowned champions but on this occasion, it was simply not to be and Manchester City retained their crown. The disappointment at missing out, however, was softened somewhat by the most amazing comeback in Anfield history (see opposite) and the prospect of a second successive Champions League final.

Barcelona (a)	CL	0-3
Newcastle United (a)	PL	3-2
Barcelona (h)	CL	4-0
Wolverhampton Wanderers (h)	PL	2-0

NEVER GIVE UP

WHEN IT COMES TO FAMOUS FOOTBALLING FIGHTBACKS IN EUROPE, LIVERPOOL SUPPORTERS COULD HAVE BEEN FORGIVEN FOR BELIEVING THEY HAD SEEN IT ALL.

A quick trawl through the club's illustrious history in continental competition will throw up many examples of how the Reds have come through against all odds.

But on the night of Tuesday 7 May 2019 they witnessed something that nobody thought possible.

Trailing 3-0 from the first leg of the Champions League semi-final against a star-studded Barcelona, Jürgen Klopp's Liverpool weren't given a chance.

To say that the majority of those who packed into Anfield for the return meeting did so more in hope than expectation would be a massive understatement.

Even to the most diehard of Reds, this seemed a lost cause – especially when it was announced that Mo Salah and Roberto Firmino would miss the game through injury.

The Champions League dream looked over for another year; plans for a trip to Madrid for the final all but scrapped.

The Liverpool crowd, however, does not give up easily and they whipped up a frenzied atmosphere to inspire the team to victory on what has since been described as arguably Anfield's greatest European night.

From the first whistle, Liverpool tore into their shell-shocked

opponents and within seven minutes the comeback had begun as Divock Origi tapped home the opening goal.

Although there was still much to do, hope had suddenly turned to belief and momentum was very much with the Reds.

When substitute Gini Wijnaldum struck twice inside three minutes to level the aggregate score early in the second-half, Barca looked a beaten side. And they soon were.

In the 79th minute, following a cleverly taken corner by Trent Alexander-Arnold, Origi slammed home his second to make it 4-0.

The unthinkable had been achieved and no-one could deny that Liverpool fully deserved this most famous of victories.

IN SUNNY SPAIN WE WON IT SIX TIMES...

1 JUNE 2019

ESTADIO METROPOLITANO, MADRID

LIVERPOOL: ALISSON, VAN DIJK, ROBERTSON, MATIP, ALEXANDER-ARNOLD, FABINHO, WIJNALDUM (MILNER), HENDERSON, FIRMINO (ORIGI), MANÉ (GOMEZ), SALAH.

TOTTENHAM HOTSPUR: LLORIS, TRIPPIER, ALDERWEIRELD, VERTONGHEN, ROSE, SISSOKO (DIER), WINKS (MOURA), ERIKSEN, ALLI (LLORENTE), SON, KANE.

REFEREE: DAMIR SKOMINA (SLOVENIA)

The silver lining to an unforgettable season came in Madrid on the first day of June 2019.

It was when five became six. An occasion to rank alongside those unforgettable European Cup winning nights of the past. 14 years and two losing finals since Liverpool were last Kings of Europe, this was truly a moment to savour.

Over 70,000 Liverpudlians had converged on the Spanish capital in an awesome show of support for Jürgen Klopp and his players. And they were rewarded by seeing their team lift the ultimate prize in European club football.

Against Tottenham Hotspur at the Estadio Metropolitano, the Reds got off to a dream start. A Sadio Mané cross was handled inside the box by Moussa Sissoko and from the resultant penalty kick Mohamed Salah netted.

Only two minutes had elapsed but further goalscoring opportunities at either end were few and far between and, as time wore on, nerves became more frayed.

Then, in the 87th minute, substitute Divock Origi took a pass from Joel Matip and drilled the ball home to eventually settle the game in Liverpool's favour, sparking delirious scenes of celebration among the players and supporters.

The demons of Kiev 12 months previous had been banished and the Reds were Champions of Europe once again. Captain Jordan Henderson had the honour of hoisting the glittering trophy aloft and the party began.

A new generation of Liverpool fans were able to experience the joy that their fathers and grandfathers had felt in 1977, 1978, 1981, 1984 and 2005. Madrid 2019 will be spoken about in the same breath as them all.

CHAMPIONS PARADE

A breath-taking reception greeted the return of the newly crowned Kings of Europe, with an estimated three quarters of a million people lining the streets of Liverpool to welcome the team home following that unforgettable night in Madrid...

FINAL

PIONS
ROPE

PLAYER PROFILES

ALISSON BECKER

Date of birth: 2 October 1992

Birthplace: Novo Hamburgo (Brazil)

Joined LFC: July 2018

Squad Number: 1

Fact: In 2018/19 Alisson completed a clean sweep of Golden Glove Awards, collecting the honour for most clean sheets in the Premier League, Champions League and Copa America.

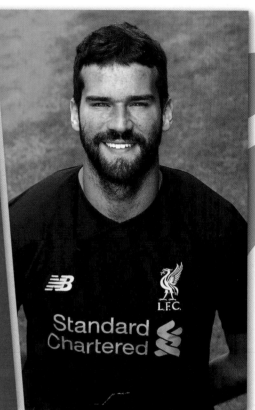

ADRIAN

Date of birth: 3 January 1987

Birthplace: Seville (Spain)

Joined LFC: August 2019

Squad Number: 13

Fact: While playing for his former club West Ham, Adrian scored the winning penalty in a shoot-out that knocked Everton out of the FA Cup in 2015.

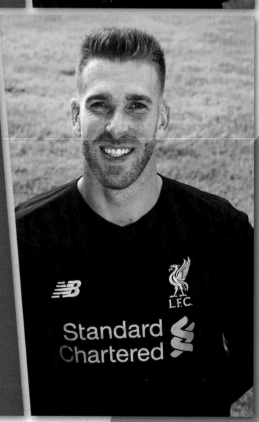

TRENT ALEXANDER-ARNOLD

Date of birth: 7 October 1998

Birthplace: Liverpool (England)

Joined LFC: 2004

Squad Number: 66

Fact: Alexander-Arnold is the youngest ever player to appear in successive Champions League finals and the youngest (excluding non-playing substitutes) to win the trophy with Liverpool.

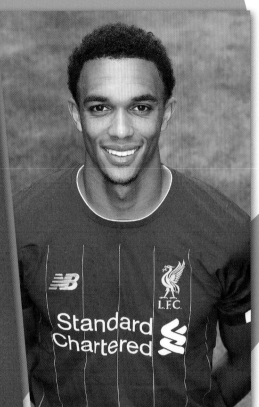

ANDY ROBERTSON

Date of birth: 11 March 1994

Birthplace: Glasgow (Scotland)

Joined LFC: July 2017

Squad Number: 26

Fact: Up until the end of the 2018/19 season Robertson had yet to be on the losing side for Liverpool in a game at Anfield.

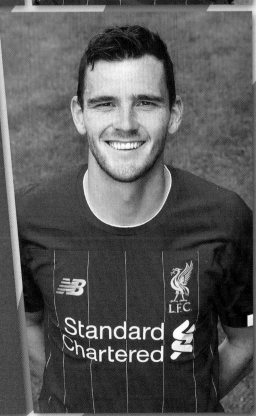

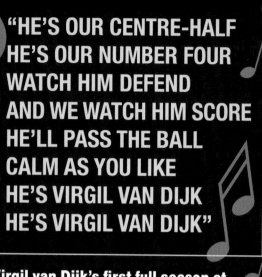

"HE'S OUR CENTRE-HALF
HE'S OUR NUMBER FOUR
WATCH HIM DEFEND
AND WE WATCH HIM SCORE
HE'LL PASS THE BALL
CALM AS YOU LIKE
HE'S VIRGIL VAN DIJK
HE'S VIRGIL VAN DIJK"

Virgil van Dijk's first full season at Anfield was a momentous one. The big Dutchman was an imperious figure at the heart of the Liverpool defence, playing an instrumental role in the club's Champions League success. As a result, he's become a cult-hero among supporters and was deservedly voted Player of the Year by his fellow professionals.

How does it feel to be the PFA Player of the Year?
"It's pretty difficult to put it into words. I think it's the highest honour you can get as a player – to be voted Player of the Year by the players you play against every week. It's special. I'm obviously very proud and honoured to win it."

In the Premier League era, only two defenders have won the award. Does that make it even more special?
"It's special, definitely. If you see the standard of strikers and playmakers we have in the league, it's unbelievable. If you see the shortlist – what kind of quality there is – it's very special that players in the league voted for me. I won't take it for granted."

Mohamed Salah won this award last year, now you. What does Jürgen Klopp do to get the best out of his players?
"He gives confidence. It's just credit to everyone who is part of Liverpool. The fans have been supporting us from day one and will always be there. Without the teammates around you, the staff, the people who work at the training ground and stadium, everyone who makes sure we're ready for the next game – everyone

is responsible for the good things going on right now at Liverpool. We just want to keep it going. Hopefully that will result in trophies in the future."

Your manager says you can get even better...
"I'm very happy with how I'm performing at the moment, how consistently I'm performing, and that I'm fit as well. I don't need to look too far ahead. I won't look too far ahead. The only goals I will set are personal goals with Liverpool."

And how does it feel to be a Champions League winner?
"Obviously, it was tough not to win the league, but to be able to get the opportunity to win this Champions League is very special. It's a beautiful trophy. Hopefully this is just the start. We have a fantastic team, who can play together for hopefully the next four or five years and build on this. Work hard and stay humble. That's the only way forward. We want to challenge for every trophy possible."

PREVIOUS WINNERS OF THE PFA PLAYER OF THE YEAR AWARD

Year	Player	Team	Year	Player	Team
1973–74	Norman Hunter	Leeds United	1996–97	Alan Shearer	Newcastle United
1974–75	Colin Todd	Derby County	1997–98	Dennis Bergkamp	Arsenal
1975–76	Pat Jennings	Tottenham Hotspur	1998–99	David Ginola	Tottenham Hotspur
1976–77	Andy Gray	Aston Villa	1999–00	Roy Keane	Manchester United
1977–78	Peter Shilton	Nottingham Forest	2000–01	Teddy Sheringham	Manchester United
1978–79	Liam Brady	Arsenal	2001–02	Ruud van Nistelrooy	Manchester United
1979–80	Terry McDermott	Liverpool	2002–03	Thierry Henry	Arsenal
1980–81	John Wark	Ipswich Town	2003–04	Thierry Henry	Arsenal
1981–82	Kevin Keegan	Southampton	2004–05	John Terry	Chelsea
1982–83	Kenny Dalglish	Liverpool	2005–06	Steven Gerrard	Liverpool
1983–84	Ian Rush	Liverpool	2006–07	Cristiano Ronaldo	Manchester United
1984–85	Peter Reid	Everton	2007–08	Cristiano Ronaldo	Manchester United
1985–86	Gary Lineker	Everton	2008–09	Ryan Giggs	Manchester United
1986–87	Clive Allen	Tottenham Hotspur	2009–10	Wayne Rooney	Manchester United
1987–88	John Barnes	Liverpool	2010–11	Gareth Bale	Tottenham Hotspur
1988–89	Mark Hughes	Manchester United	2011–12	Robin van Persie	Arsenal
1989–90	David Platt	Aston Villa	2012–13	Gareth Bale	Tottenham Hotspur
1990–91	Mark Hughes	Manchester United	2013–14	Luis Suárez	Liverpool
1991–92	Gary Pallister	Manchester United	2014–15	Eden Hazard	Chelsea
1992–93	Paul McGrath	Aston Villa	2015–16	Riyad Mahrez	Leicester City
1993–94	Eric Cantona	Manchester United	2016–17	N'Golo Kanté	Chelsea
1994–95	Alan Shearer	Blackburn Rovers	2017–18	Mohamed Salah	Liverpool
1995–96	Les Ferdinand	Newcastle United	2018–19	Virgil van Dijk	Liverpool

- Van Dijk is the seventh Liverpool player to be crowned Player of the Year by the PFA, following in the footsteps of Terry McDermott, Kenny Dalglish, Ian Rush, John Barnes, Steven Gerrard and Mohamed Salah.

- He is also one of only six defenders to have won the award, joining Norman Hunter (Leeds United 1973/74), Colin Todd (Derby County 1974/75), Gary Pallister (Manchester United 1991/92), Paul McGrath (Aston Villa 1992/93) and John Terry (Chelsea 2004/05).

- Van Dijk saw off competition from fellow Red Sadio Mané, Manchester City trio Sergio Aguero, Bernardo Silva and Raheem Sterling, and Chelsea forward Eden Hazard to scoop the accolade.

- He was also named in the PFA Premier League Team of the Year for 2018-19, alongside three of his Liverpool team-mates; Trent Alexander-Arnold, Sadio Mané and Andy Robertson.

VVD'S VITAL STATS 2018/19

4,465 Minutes played for Liverpool in all competitions this season - more than any other outfield player in the squad.

3,471 Touches in the Premier League. Only Chelsea's Jorginho (3,551) had more.

3,385 Minutes played in the Premier League this season, out of a maximum of 3,420.

3,037 Passes made in the top flight. Only Jorginho has attempted more.

257 Clearances made across all competitions - the most of any LFC player and more than double his nearest rival, Joel Matip (118).

199 Clearances made in the Premier League - a top 10 ranking.

182 Aerial battles won in the top flight - a top 10 ranking.

112 Headed clearances in the league - a top 10 ranking.

97 Total shots on target faced by Liverpool in the Premier League - only Manchester City are more miserly, with 83.

74.9% of aerial battles won by van Dijk - the best in the Premier League (minimum of 200 aerials).

50 Appearances for Liverpool this term from a possible 53 games.

38 Games won across all competitions.

25 Clean sheets in all competitions.

6 Goals scored.

KLOPP ON VVD

"I'm really proud it's the second time in a row I can speak about a wonderful player who won the award for Player of the Season: Virgil van Dijk. Who would have thought that when he started back in Holland? I think not everybody saw immediately what kind of player hides in this giant body. But now the whole world is aware of that and I'm really happy I can be a little bit around that development. I would love to think it's because of me! But obviously it's not; he was already the player he is now when we bought him from Southampton. It all worked out. From the first moment I was so excited about the opportunity to work together and now you are the man – at least for this season!"

22 Premier League goals conceded by Liverpool this season - fewer than any other team in the top flight.

5 Number of outfield players in the Premier League with more minutes this season.

1 Substitution.

4 Assists provided.

0.58 Average goals conceded by Liverpool per Premier League match - the best record in the top flight.

KINGS OF EUROPE WORDSEARCH

THE PLAYERS BELOW WILL GO DOWN IN HISTORY AS HAVING ALL PLAYED A PART IN LIVERPOOL'S VICTORIOUS CHAMPIONS LEAGUE WINNING CAMPAIGN OF 2018/19. SEE IF YOU CAN FIND THEM BY SEARCHING THE GRID VERTICALLY, HORIZONTALLY OR DIAGONALLY…

```
F F K D X M C Z E M S M V Z D
M M X H M Q Y T N H O Q Q L X
Y M Q A M K B L A M B R O R N
L P T C O X E Q M R G N E M Z
V I R V B N I I E N R B T N X
P L N A K R I N T A E H K Z O
O A O N I K L M R A A R L L L
H L S D G I T E R L B F V N K
N L S I M D D N A I J X H O K
I A I J L N D S M P F F B Y L
B N L K A R O B E R T S O N L
A A A X T M U D L A N J I W J
F H E N D E R S O N G K T N Q
T L E G D I R R U T S J R H H
A Z E M O G K H M O R I G I B
```

ALEXANDER-ARNOLD	HENDERSON	MATIP	SALAH
ALISSON	KEITA	MILNER	SHAQIRI
FABINHO	LALLANA	MORENO	STURRIDGE
FIRMINO	LOVREN	ORIGI	VAN DIJK

THE ORIGINAL 'PINSTRIPE REDS' 1982-1985

PINSTRIPES ON LIVERPOOL'S HOME SHIRT ARE NOTHING NEW.

The kit Jürgen Klopp's team are sporting for the 2019/20 season is a throwback to the one worn by the players who served under Bob Paisley and Joe Fagan in the early-to-mid 1980s.

But while the current strip has been warmly welcomed by supporters since its release, those thin vertical lines of white were not always quite so popular.

When first added to the proud all-red shirt in August 1982, they were viewed as a radical modification of the traditional design and not greeted with universal approval by Kopites of the time.

However, Liverpool fans soon grew to love them and it's a shirt that now evokes fond memories of a golden era…

Some of the club's greatest players wor

Many famous games were played in it

Spectacular goals scored in it

And momentous victories achieved in it...
Two league titles, two League Cups and a European Cup...

PLAYER PROFILES

VIRGIL VAN DIJK

Date of birth: 8 July 1991

Birthplace: Breda (The Netherlands)

Joined LFC: January 2018

Squad Number: 4

Fact: No opposition player managed to dribble the ball past van Dijk in any of his 50 appearances for Liverpool during the 2018/19 season.

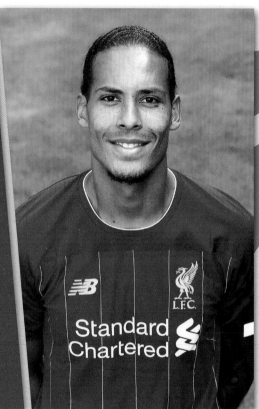

JOE GOMEZ

Date of birth: 23 May 1997

Birthplace: Catford (England)

Joined LFC: June 2015

Squad Number: 12

Fact: Gomez has represented England at every level and was part of the squad that won the UEFA European Under-17 Championship in 2014.

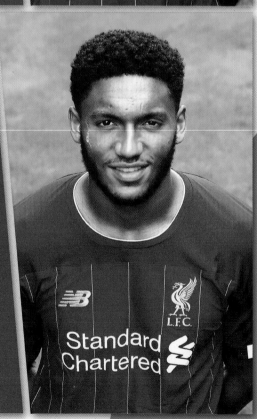

JOEL MATIP

Date of birth: 8 August 1991

Birthplace: Bochum (Germany)

Joined LFC: July 2016

Squad Number: 32

Fact: Matip's first assist in a Liverpool shirt was the pass from which Divock Origi scored in the 2019 Champions League final.

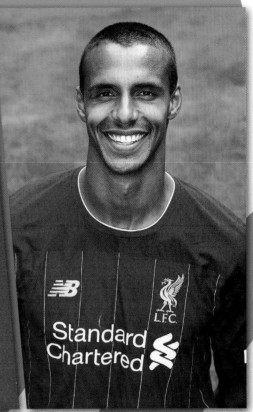

DEJAN LOVREN

Date of birth: 5 July 1989

Birthplace: Zenica (Serbia)

Joined LFC: July 2014

Squad Number: 6

Fact: Lovren is one of only five Liverpool players to have played in a World Cup final.

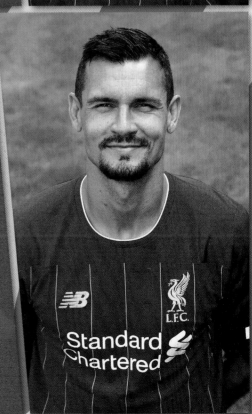

BACK OF THE NET

LIVERPOOL SCORED A TOTAL OF 115 GOALS DURING THE COURSE OF THE 2018/19 SEASON. WE'VE PICKED OUT 10 OF THE MOST MEMORABLE BUT WHAT WERE YOUR PERSONAL FAVOURITES?

FIRMINO V PSG (H) 18/9/2018

STURRIDGE V CHELSEA (A) 29/9/2018

ORIGI V EVERTON (H) 2/12/2018

FIRMINO V ARSENAL (H) 29/12/2018

MANÉ V BAYERN MUNICH (A) 13/3/2019

SALAH V SOUTHAMPTON (A) 5/4/2019

SALAH V CHELSEA (H) 14/4/2019

WIJNALDUM V CARDIFF CITY (A) 21/4/2019

ORIGI V BARCELONA (H) 7/5/2019

ORIGI V TOTTENHAM (CL FINAL) 1/6/2019

MY TOP 10 LFC GOALS OF 2018/19

1. _____
2. _____
3. _____
4. _____
5. _____
6. _____
7. _____
8. _____
9. _____
10. _____

SADIO MANÉ: A DAY IN HIS LIFE

AN INTRIGUING INSIGHT INTO THE DAILY ROUTINES AND MINDSET OF LIVERPOOL'S SENEGAL STAR SADIO MANÉ…

'This is my dream, this is something I've always wanted to do, and I am so grateful that I am able to do it now.'

MORNING

I've always been someone who wakes up early, and as soon as I do, I'll take a shower and then pray. The same routine, every single day. After that, depends on what time our training is for the day. If our report time is 9.30am, for example, I still like to come in a little bit earlier and get some treatment. I'll always arrive earlier than report time, sometimes up to an hour before, so I can get treatment with the medical staff and then go into the gym and get myself ready for the day's session.

If it is an early report, I'll have breakfast at Melwood, but most of the time I'll eat at home before I head in. It's different what I have each day, really; some days I'll have nuts with yoghurt and fruit, sometimes it is eggs with bread, or sometimes it is porridge. I don't have a particular favourite food in general. The only rule I have is I always need to eat healthy. It is so important.

DRESSING ROOM

We have a good relationship as a squad. I have been here three years and some players have come in since and are new, but it's like we've been together since my first year here. This is something that makes Liverpool special, I think. Who is the loudest? Robbo, always! He is always, talking. You might think he is quiet, but he is always talking, always joking, talking loudly, everything!

TRAINING

Of course, training is sometimes very hard, but when it's hard in training I think that will ultimately make things easier in a game. That's why I think if we play at a high tempo, it's difficult for any team to play against us because of the training, so we actually enjoy the intensity of it.

AFTERNOON/EVENING

Once training is over, I usually go home and chill for the evening, although sometimes I'll go to a restaurant. At home, I'll sometimes have my friends over and we'll play games – not video games, mainly board games. We'll also watch series or movies together. We'll also watch any live football that's on. The friends who will come over to my house are ones I've known for a while – people I know from Southampton, from Paris and, of course, some friends from Liverpool. Naby is also someone who will sometimes come over to my house.

Every day, at 7.30pm I will eat my evening meal. Again, as long as it is a healthy meal then for me, mentally, it is top. After that, sometimes I will look at social media, but not always. In this generation, most people have a smart phone and are on social media, but I don't like to post too much – although I probably post a little bit more on Instagram.

One thing I do every single day, however, is speak with my mum, my uncle and my sisters. They live back home, so I always speak to them on the phone. In the beginning, I used to miss home a lot - really, really missed it - but now, I know Europe, I am here, I am working and I am used to it. If I am going back home, I am very excited to be going back because it's my home country and I love it, but when I am here and working, I don't feel nostalgic or miss home.

PRE-MATCH

Obviously as footballers we spend a lot of time in hotels, but I don't mind it. I am used to it now. Maybe it makes you more concentrated, so I think that's important. When we are staying away, I'll eat in the hotel and then go to my room, watch a movie or a TV series on my iPad and then go to bed. I sleep very well – but I sleep very well every single time, whether it's a hotel or at home. The latest I like to go to bed is midnight, but usually it's 11pm for me so I am feeling well rested the next day.

MATCHDAY

On the day of a game, from the moment I wake up, I like to make sure I'm relaxed and focused on the match. I am someone who is always looking forward.

In the beginning, I had some nerves on matchdays, but now I am more focused on the game, thinking about how I can have a great game in my mind. I don't have nervous feelings.

I don't have any particular rituals before a match. I just go there, feel relaxed and try to win the game – and when we travel to the stadiums on the coach, I am not doing much. Maybe playing on my phone, listening to music.

I've always been able to stay very focused before matches. If I want to focus, I just focus and block everything else out.

The dressing room is always different on a matchday. At Melwood you can joke around, but on game day you can't because people like to focus on the game, so they like to be calm and prepare for the game. I'll do some pre-activation work, some stretching and then when it's time, go to warm up.

DURING THE MATCH

Once it comes to the game itself, the feeling when you walk out of the tunnel is one of excitement for the game: you can't wait for it. Scoring a goal? How it feels depends – sometimes you can score the winning goal, the equaliser or score at 2-0 up or 3-0 down, so it feels different. A winning goal is always more exciting and a better feeling, but scoring a goal is always special – and even better if it's helped us to win the match.

POST-MATCH

After a game, I will have an ice bath and a massage if there's enough time, then I'll go home, eat, watch movies until I fall asleep. I am someone who likes to sleep early and always sleeps well, but this doesn't happen after a night game! Sometimes I'll only be able to sleep around three, maybe four hours, maximum at night because of adrenaline. I'm used to it, though, so it's fine. I'll just watch films or series until I fall asleep.

PLAYER PROFILES

JAMES MILNER

Date of birth: 4 January 1986

Birthplace: Horsforth (England)

Joined LFC: July 2015

Squad Number: 7

Fact: Milner has scored more penalties (16) for Liverpool than any other player currently at the club.

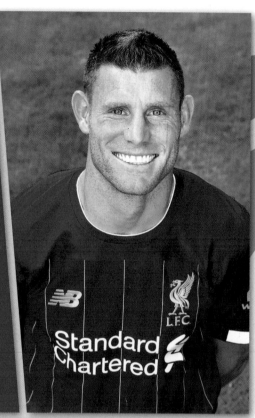

FABINHO

Date of birth: 23 October 1993

Birthplace: Campinas (Brazil)

Joined LFC: July 2018

Squad Number: 3

Fact: In 2018/19, his debut season at the club, Fabinho made more tackles than any other Liverpool midfielder.

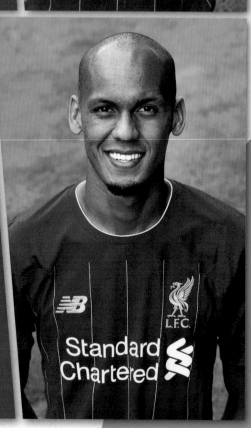

JORDAN HENDERSON

Date of birth: 17 June 1990

Birthplace: Sunderland (England)

Joined LFC: June 2011

Squad Number: 14

Fact: Henderson is the fifth Liverpool captain to lift the European Cup/Champions League – following in the footsteps of Emlyn Hughes (twice), Phil Thompson, Graeme Souness and Steven Gerrard.

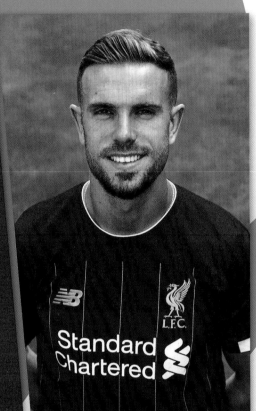

GEORGINIO WIJNALDUM

Date of birth: 11 November 1990

Birthplace: Rotterdam (The Netherlands)

Joined LFC: July 2016

Squad Number: 5

Fact: Wijnaldum hadn't scored an away goal for Liverpool until the 2018 Champions League semi-final second leg in Rome.

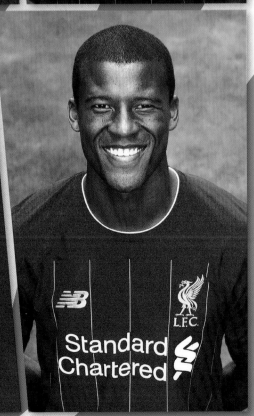

CUP GLORY FOR LIVERPOOL YOUNGSTERS

LIVERPOOL WON THE PRESTIGIOUS FA YOUTH CUP FOR A FOURTH TIME IN 2019 AND DID SO IN DRAMATIC FASHION.

It was the club's first success in the competition since 2007 and a well-deserved triumph for the young Reds.

Under the guidance of coach Barry Lewtas, they made impressive progress through the early rounds; even though it required a stoppage-time winner from Bobby Duncan for them to clear the first hurdle, at home to Portsmouth.

Comfortable victories over Accrington Stanley – with captain Paul Glatzel grabbing a hat-trick – and Wigan Athletic came next, before an emphatic 5-1 win away to Bury in the quarter-final.

Anfield was the venue for the semi-final against Watford and the prolific Glatzel struck a memorable brace in front of the Kop to secure Liverpool's first final appearance for ten years.

Only Manchester City now stood in their way but, with home advantage having been conceded, the odds were stacked heavily against the Reds' Academy starlets, especially after they fell behind to the opening goal on the stroke of half-time.

It looked like the winner but with just four minutes left on the clock the never-say-die spirit of this Liverpool team prevailed when Duncan hit a spectacular long-range equaliser.

Extra-time brought no further goals and in the nail-biting shoot-out that followed it was the Liverpool penalty-takers who held their nerve best.

Neco Williams, Elijah Dixon-Bonner, Abdi Sharif, Jack Bearne and Glatzel all converted from the spot to clinch victory and add a silver lining to what had been a memorable season for Lewtas' team.

The road to FA Youth Cup glory 2018/19

3rd round: Portsmouth (h) 3-2
Goalscorers: Duncan (2), Sharif

4th round: Accrington Stanley (h) 4-0
Goalscorers: Williams, Glatzel (3)

5th round: Wigan Athletic (h) 2-0
Goalscorers: Glatzel, Duncan

Quarter-final: Bury (a) 5-1
Goalscorers: Glatzel (2), Cain, Williams, Duncan

Semi-final: Watford (h) 2-1
Goalscorers: Glatzel (2)

Final: Manchester City (a) 1-1, won 5-3 on pens
Goalscorers: Duncan (penalties: N Williams, Dixon-Bonner, Sharif, Bearne, Glatzel)

Liverpool's previous FA Youth Cup victories

1996 – West Ham United 4-1 on aggregate

2006 – Manchester City 3-2 on aggregate

2007 – Manchester United 2-2 on aggregate (won 4-3 on pens)

Bury

Liverpool's victorious 2019 FA Youth Cup winning squad

Player	Games	Goals*
Rhys Williams (defender)	6	2
Leighton Clarkson (midfieler)	6	0
Elijaha Dixon-Bonner (midfielder)	6	0
Paul Glatzel (forward)	6	8
Bobby Duncan (forward)	6	5
Abdi Sharif (midfield)	6	1
Viteslav Jaros (goalkeeper)	5	0
Morgan Boyes (defender)	5	0
Jake Cain (midfielder)	5	1
Yasser Larouci (midfielder)	5	0
Jack Walls (defender)	4	0
Jack Bearne (forward)	4	0
Luis Longstaff (midfielder)	4	0
Neco Williams (defender)	3	0
Remi Savage (defender)	2	0
Fidel O'Rourke (forward)	2	0
Tom Clayton (defender)	1	0
Matteo Ritaccio (midfielder)	1	0
Edvard Tagseth (midfielder)	1	0
Luca Ashby-Hammond (goalkeeper)	1	0
Niall Brookwell (unused substitute)		
Oscar Kelly (unused substitute)		

*(not including penalties in shoot-outs)

Watford

Manchester City

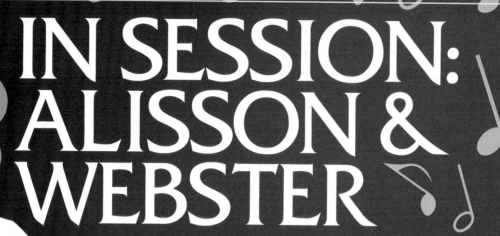

IN SESSION: ALISSON & WEBSTER

ALISSON BECKER'S LOVE OF MUSIC IS NO SECRET. NOR IS THE TALENT OF RISING LIVERPUDLIAN MUSICIAN JAMIE WEBSTER. SO, WHEN THE PAIR OF THEM MET UP AT DISTRICT, THE CITY CENTRE VENUE WHERE WEBSTER REGULARLY HEADLINES THE INCREASINGLY POPULAR BOSS NIGHT EVENTS, LIVERPOOL'S NUMBER ONE SWAPPED HIS GOALKEEPING GLOVES FOR A GUITAR. AND AS WELL AS PLAYING A FEW TUNES TOGETHER, A FASCINATING CHAT ABOUT THEIR SHARED PASSIONS ENSUED…

JW: Shall we go and play some music?

AB: Yeah, of course. Two guitars, yeah.

JW: Well, I'll let you have the good guitar.

AB: No, you take it.

JW: No, you take it, because you've got safer hands than me!

 Allez, allez, allez
Allez, allez, allez
Allez, allez, allez
Allez, allez, allez

JW: What songs have you been playing lately?

AB: Now, in the moment, Baby Shark is the best one. My daughter, always when I come home to play with her, she takes my guitar, gives it to me, I start to play and she starts to dance.

JW: When new players come to Liverpool, as part of their initiation, they have to sing a song. Didn't you come in with a guitar? What song did you play?

AB: Yeah. I played a Brazilian song, but we had the karaoke (too). And in the karaoke I sang an Oasis song… Don't Look Back In Anger.

JW: What sort of music do you normally listen to?

AB: I listen a lot to sertanejo, it's like country music, in Brazil it's very popular. And, 'Allez, Allez, Allez!' Every game I listen to this. It's very nice.

JW: Thank you very much. Well, hopefully we'll have a song about you soon. What do you think?

AB: Yeah, it would be nice, but I need to take some time, I know how the thing works. I'll try to give you motivation for one.

JW: To be honest, that save against Napoli, think that's all the motivation anyone needs, mate. What about something like..

Alisson's our goalie,
the best there is around

And Robbo is the greatest
that Jürgen ever found

Virgil is our favourite,
a wizard of the game...

And here's the mighty Salah
to do it once again

We love you, Liverpool, we do

We love you, Liverpool, we do

We love you, Liverpool, we do

Ohhh, Liverpool, we love you.

JW: Something like that?

AB: Fantastic, mate, fantastic. Now tell me about the events that you do with the fans here…

JW: There's an event called BOSS Nights, it started about 8 to 10 years ago, maybe 50 people coming down after the match to listen to a bit of music, it's just got bigger and bigger over the years, so now we do it in here at District. The atmosphere's great in here.

AB: Are you not a professional singer?

JW: I mean, I don't do it full time, I'm an electrician 9-5, but hopefully one day. I'm going to release my own music so if you want to play some guitar on that let me know and we'll get in the studio.

AB: Why are you a Liverpool fan?

JW: As you know, same in your country, it's things that have been passed down through the families. You look at the videos of years ago and the great nights Liverpool Football Club have had, and you just think, "That's something I want to be part of," you know? I've been following Liverpool home and away and in Europe since I was old enough to pay for it myself, so since I started work, maybe eight years now.

AB: You come to every game now?

JW: Yeah, home and away, all the time. So if there's ever a seat on the coach, let me know!

AB: This is the same in our country, you take the tradition of the same team as your dad, your mum, it's nice. My team is Internacional. It's very passionate over there. The supporters are very crazy.

JW: So obviously, Roma, in Italy, the fans are very passionate, aren't they? How different was it for you, obviously last season, being at Anfield, on the opposition team?

AB: It was difficult playing against Liverpool, the quality of the team is amazing, and then the 12th player, outside the pitch, that is the supporters. Last year I can remember the semi-finals. It was difficult, the atmosphere was incredible. I like to play with the supporters from the other team shouting, talking to me…but here was something different.

JW: After seeing that, when you came to Liverpool, was that something you were looking forward to?

AB: When I signed, when I wanted to come here and I knew about the interest of Liverpool, yeah, for sure. We players, we search for a team who wants you, a team with quality, with a good manager, and with great supporters, and I think here at Liverpool we have maybe the biggest supporters in the world.

JW: Is there a feeling you've got with this team that you've maybe never had with anyone else?

AB: Yeah, I think we can do something special here, but we need to keep our feet on the ground and keep working, working, working.

JW: How big a part do you think the fans can play in that?

AB: Yeah, I think the supporters are a great part of this team, they cannot go to the pitch and play, but they all want to. They can do something to move us, to charge us, so we can do something more on the pitch.

JW: That's brilliant. How long have you been speaking English, by the way? Because your English is very good.

AB: I always watched movies in English with subtitles, music in English, so it's not too difficult for me, study a little bit, talking every day, practising.

JW: Do you find it harder speaking to someone maybe from Liverpool than someone from somewhere else in England?

AB: Yeah. But if you speak slowly, I can understand.

JW: You've done very well with me anyway. The Scouse. Happy days. Thanks again, man.

Li-ver-pool, Li-ver-pool, la-la-la
Li-ver-pool, Li-ver-pool...

WHEN WE WERE YOUNG

Can you identify these current Liverpool players and tell us at which club they started their professional careers?

A.

B.

C.

D.

CLUB:

PLAYER:

CLUB:

PLAYER:

CLUB:

PLAYER:

CLUB:

PLAYER:

PLAYER PROFILES

NABY KEITA

Date of birth: 10 February 1995

Birthplace: Conakry (Guinea)

Joined LFC: July 2018

Squad Number: 8

Fact: Keita's goal against Huddersfield in April 2019 is the fastest ever scored by Liverpool in the Premier League – it was timed at 15 seconds.

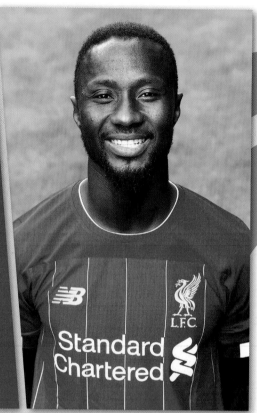

ADAM LALLANA

Date of birth: 10 May 1988

Birthplace: St Albans (England)

Joined LFC: July 2014

Squad Number: 20

Fact: Lallana has been named in the PFA Team of the Year at League One, Championship and Premier League level.

ALEX OXLADE-CHAMBERLAIN

Date of birth: 15 August 1993

Birthplace: Portsmouth (England)

Joined LFC: August 2017

Squad Number: 15

Fact: When Oxlade-Chamberlain netted for Arsenal against Olympiacos in September 2011 he became the youngest English player to score in the Champions League.

XHERDAN SHAQIRI

Date of birth: 10 October 1991

Birthplace: Gjilan (Kosovo)

Joined LFC: July 2018

Squad Number: 23

Fact: Shaqiri is the only player in Liverpool's squad to own two Champions League winners medals – he won the first with Bayern Munich in 2014.

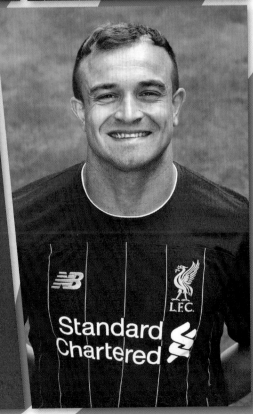

LIVERPOOL'S LAST CHAMPIONS

APRIL 2020 WILL MARK THE 30TH ANNIVERSARY OF LIVERPOOL'S 18TH LEAGUE TITLE TRIUMPH. HOPEFULLY THE NEXT ONE IS NOT TOO FAR AWAY BUT, IN THE MEANTIME, WE REMEMBER THE MEN WHO HELPED MAKE HISTORY FOR THE CLUB THREE DECADES AGO...

KENNY DALGLISH

Player/manager. 1 appearance. 0 goals.
Born: Glasgow, 4/3/1951
Joined LFC: August 1977 from Celtic

ALAN HANSEN

Defender & Captain. 31 appearances. 0 goals.
Born: Sauchie, 13/6/1955
Joined LFC: May 1977 from Partick Thistle

BRUCE GROBBELAAR

Goalkeeper. 38 appearances. 0 goals.
Born: Durban (South Africa), 6/10/1957
Joined LFC: March 1981 from Vancouver Whitecaps

STEVE STAUNTON

Defender. 20 appearances. 0 goals.
Born: Drogheda, 19/1/1969
Joined LFC: September 1986 from Dundalk

STEVE NICOL

Defender. 23 appearances. 6 goals.
Born: Ayrshire, 11/12/1961
Joined LFC: October 1981 from Ayr United

GLENN HYSEN

Defender. 35 appearances. 1 goal.
Born: Gothenburg (Sweden), 30/10/1959
Joined LFC: June 1989 from Fiorentina

BARRY VENISON

Defender. 25 appearances. 0 goals.
Born: Consett, 16/8/1964
Joined LFC: July 1986 from Sunderland

GARY GILLESPIE

Defender. 13 appearances. 4 goals.
Born: Stirling, 5/7/1960
Joined LFC: July 1983 from Coventry City

DAVID BURROWS

Defender. 26 appearances. 0 goals.
Born: Dudley, 25/10/1968
Joined LFC: October 1988 from West Bromwich Albion

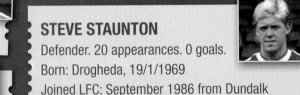

GARY ABLETT
Defender. 15 appearances. 0 goals.
Born: Liverpool, 19/11/1965
Joined LFC: October 1981 from schoolboy

JOHN BARNES

Midfielder/Forward. 34 appearances. 22 goals.
Born: Kingston (Jamaica), 7/11/1963
Joined LFC: June 1987 from Watford

NICK TANNER
Defender. 4 appearances. 0 goals.
Born: Bristol, 24/5/1965
Joined LFC: July 1988 from Bristol Rovers

RAY HOUGHTON
Midfielder. 19 appearances. 1 goal.
Born: Glasgow, 9/1/1962
Joined LFC: October 1987 from Oxford United

MIKE MARSH

Midfielder. 2 appearances. 0 goals.
Born: Liverpool, 21/7/1969
Joined LFC: August 1987 from Kirkby Town

RONNY ROSENTHAL
Forward. 8 appearances. 7 goals.
Born: Haifa (Israel), 11/10/1963
Joined LFC: March 1990 from Standard Liege

STEVE MCMAHON

Midfielder. 38 appearances. 5 goals.
Born: Liverpool, 20/8/1961
Joined LFC: September 1985 from Aston Villa

PETER BEARDSLEY

Forward. 29 appearances. 10 goals.
Born: Newcastle, 18/1/1961
Joined LFC: July 1987 from Newcastle United

JAN MOLBY
Midfielder. 17 appearances. 1 goal.
Born: Kolding (Denmark), 4/7/1963
Joined LFC: August 1984 from Ajax

IAN RUSH

Forward. 36 appearances. 18 goals.
Born: St Asaph, 20/10/1961
Joined LFC: August 1988 from Juventus

RONNIE WHELAN

Midfielder. 34 appearances. 1 goal.
Born: Dublin, 25/9/1961
Joined LFC: September 1979 from Home Farm

JOHN ALDRIDGE
Forward. 2 appearances. 1 goal.
Born: Liverpool, 18/9/1958
Joined LFC: January 1987 from Oxford United

1989/90 FACTS & FIGURES

 Half the clubs that made up the First Division in 1989/90 are no longer in the top-flight

 The cheapest priced ticket at Anfield was just £4, while a matchday programme would have cost you £1

 And seven of the away grounds Liverpool visited in the league that season have since been demolished

 There was no Bill Shankly statue or Paisley Gates

Live football on television was a rarity, with only seven of Liverpool's 38 games being shown in full

 The Kop was still terracing, while the Main Stand, Anfield Road and Kemlyn Road all comprised of just one tier

 There was no LFCTV or Sky Sports News…no Twitter, Facebook or Instagram

 Liverpool also recorded…

 And 3pm kick-offs on a Saturday afternoon were the norm

- the biggest away win (6-1 at Coventry on the final day)
- the most wins (23)
- the fewest defeats (5)
- the highest number of goals scored (78)
- and the lowest number of goals conceded (37)

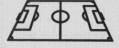 Anfield's capacity in 1989/90 was just over 38,000, with the average attendance for league games being 36,873

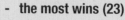

 And the club were on course for the double until losing 4-3 to Crystal Palace in the FA Cup semi-final

 Ronny Rosenthal scored three away to Charlton in his first full game

 On 12 September that season Liverpool defeated Crystal Palace 9-0

In the above game eight different players got on the scoresheet

It was the biggest home win by any team in the division that season

 John Aldridge scored a penalty with his first touch of the ball in his last game

Kenny Dalglish, Alan Hansen and John Aldridge all made their final appearances for Liverpool this season

Glenn Hysen, Nick Tanner and Ronny Rosenthal made their debuts

Three different players captained the Reds (Hansen, Whelan & McMahon)

Current Match of the Day presenter Gary Lineker was the First Division's top goalscorer with 24 goals for Tottenham Hotspur

But the Football Writers' Player of the Year accolade deservedly went to Liverpool number ten John Barnes

Liverpool's title win of 1989/90 was the club's 10th in 15 years

Captain Alan Hansen had been involved in eight of them, equalling the club record set by Phil Neal

It was also the fifth and last major trophy won during the managerial reign of Kenny Dalglish

John Barnes was Liverpool's top scorer with 22 goals

Liverpool's heaviest defeat was a 4-1 loss to Southampton at The Dell

Bruce Grobbelaar and Steve McMahon were the only two players to feature in every league game

First Division League table 1989/90

1	LIVERPOOL	38	23	10	5	78	37	79
2	Aston Villa	38	21	7	10	57	38	70
3	Tottenham Hotspur	38	19	6	13	59	47	63
4	Arsenal	38	18	8	12	54	38	62
5	Chelsea	38	16	12	10	58	50	60
6	Everton	38	17	8	13	57	46	59
7	Southampton	38	15	10	13	71	63	55
8	Wimbledon	38	13	16	9	47	40	55
9	Nottingham Forest	38	15	9	14	55	47	54
10	Norwich City	38	13	14	11	44	42	53
11	Queens Park Rangers	38	13	11	14	45	44	50
12	Coventry City	38	14	7	17	39	59	49
13	Manchester United	38	13	9	16	46	47	48
14	Manchester City	38	12	12	14	43	52	48
15	Crystal Palace	38	13	9	16	42	66	48
16	Derby County	38	13	7	18	43	40	46
17	Luton Town	38	10	13	15	43	57	43
18	Sheffield Wednesday	38	11	10	17	35	51	43
19	Charlton Athletic	38	7	9	22	31	57	30
20	Millwall	38	5	11	22	39	65	26

STAT-ATTACK

ALL THE NEED-TO-KNOW FACTS AND FIGURES ABOUT LIVERPOOL'S 2018/19 SEASON…

Team Stats
Premier League/
Champions League

Stat	PL	CL
Games played	38	13
Goals scored	89	24
Goals per game	2.34	1.85
Total shots	134	141
Shooting accuracy	52.1	41.1%
Goals from inside the box	84	24
Goals from outside the box	5	0
Goals direct from free kicks	1	0
Penalties	7	5
Goals conceded	22	12
Goals conceded per game	0.58	0.92
Clean sheets	21	6
Clearances	639	218
Tackles	609	226
Percentage of tackles won	61.58%	58.85%
Blocks	708	20
Duels won	50.4%	49.8%
Aerial duels won	50.7	49.6%
Average possession	62%	52%
Passing accuracy	84.5%	79.9%
Percentage of long passes	9.5%	11.6%
Total crosses	487	150
Successful crosses	99	37
Fouls won	347	123
Fouls against	315	157
Penalties conceded	1	0
Yellow cards	37	21
Red cards	2	0

Appearances
(all competitions)

Player	Appearances
Mohamed Salah	52
Alisson Becker	51
Sadio Mané	50
Virgil van Dijk	50
Roberto Firmino	48
Andy Robertson	48
Georginio Wijnaldum	47
James Milner	45
Jordan Henderson	44
Fabinho	41
Trent Alexander-Arnold	40
Naby Keïta	33
Joel Matip	31
Xherdan Shaqiri	30
Daniel Sturridge	27
Joe Gomez	25
Divock Origi	21
Dejan Lovren	18
Adam Lallana	16
Nathaniel Clyne	5
Alberto Moreno	5
Rafael Camacho	2
Simon Mignolet	2
Alex Oxlade-Chamberlain	2
Ki-Jana Hoever	1
Curtis Jones	1

Goals
(all competitions)

Player	Goals
Mohamed Salah	27
Sadio Mané	26
Roberto Firmino	16
James Milner	7
Divock Origi	7
Xherdan Shaqiri	6
Virgil van Dijk	6
Georginio Wijnaldum	5
Daniel Sturridge	4
Naby Keïta	3
Own goal	3
Trent Alexander-Arnold	1
Fabinho	1
Jordan Henderson	1
Dejan Lovren	1
Joel Matip	1

Assists
(all competitions)

Player	Goals
Trent Alexander-Arnold	17
Andy Robertson	13
Mohamed Salah	13
Roberto Firmino	7
James Milner	6
Sadio Mané	5
Xherdan Shaqiri	5
Jordan Henderson	4
Virgil van Dijk	4
Fabinho	2
Daniel Sturridge	2
Naby Keïta	3
Dejan Lovren	1
Joel Matip	1
Divock Origi	1
Georginio Wijnaldum	1

Individual Awards

PFA Player of the Year
Virgil van Dijk

Premier League Player of the Year
Virgil van Dijk

UEFA Men's Player of the Year
Virgil van Dijk

Premier League Golden Boot
Mohamed Salah & Sadio Mané
(shared with Arsenal's Pierre-Emerick Aubameyang)

LFC Standard Chartered Player of the Month
August – Virgil van Dijk
September – Daniel Sturridge
October – Mohamed Salah
November – Trent Alexander-Arnold
December – Mohamed Salah
January – Sadio Mané
February – Virgil van Dijk
March – Sadio Mané
April – Mohamed Salah

Premier League Player of the Month
December – Virgil van Dijk
March – Sadio Mané

Premier League Manager of the Month
December & March – Jürgen Klopp

Premier League Golden Glove
Alisson Becker

Champions League Goalkeeper of the Season
Alisson Becker

Champions League Defender of the Season
Virgil van Dijk

PLAYER PROFILES

ROBERTO FIRMINO

Date of birth: 2 October 1991

Birthplace: Maceio (Brazil)

Joined LFC: July 2015

Squad Number: 9

Fact: Firmino is the only player to have started in all four of the cup finals reached by Liverpool since Jürgen Klopp became manager.

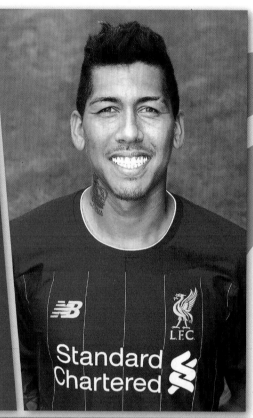

SADIO MANÉ

Date of birth: 10 April 1992

Birthplace: Sedhiou (Senegal)

Joined LFC: June 2016

Squad Number: 10

Fact: In 2015 Mané scored the fastest hat-trick in Premier League history, netting three times for Southampton against Aston Villa in just two minutes and 56 seconds.

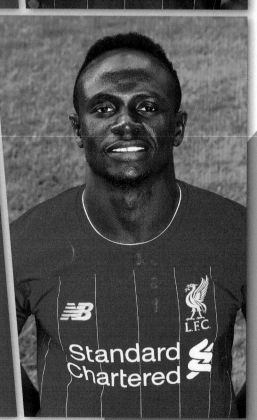

MOHAMED SALAH

Date of birth: 15 June 1992

Birthplace: Basyoun (Egypt)

Joined LFC: July 2017

Squad Number: 11

Fact: The 44 goals scored by Salah in 2017/18 is most by a Liverpool player in his debut season with the club.

DIVOCK ORIGI

Date of birth: 18 April 1995

Birthplace: Ostend (Belgium)

Joined LFC: July 2014

Squad Number: 27

Fact: During the 2018/19 Champions League campaign, Origi had just three shots on target but scored with every one of them – twice against Barcelona in the semi-final and once against Tottenham in the final.

LIVERPOOL'S GOLDEN SAMBAS

JUST SIX WEEKS AFTER WINNING THE CHAMPIONS LEAGUE WITH LIVERPOOL, ROBERTO FIRMINO AND ALISSON BECKER EXPERIENCED THE THRILL OF LIFTING A MAJOR TROPHY ALL OVER AGAIN.

This time it was back in their home country as part of Brazil's victorious 2019 Copa America team.

The Reds pair were key members of the Selecao side throughout the prestigious tournament, featuring in all six games for the hosts as they claimed the title for a 9th time.

Firmino, Brazil's first-choice centre forward, netted two goals, including the crucial strike that sealed victory over Argentina in the semi-final.

Alisson, meanwhile, was his formidable self between the sticks and conceded just one goal – a penalty in the final against Peru at the Maracana.

For both players, it was the first senior international honour of their careers and they follow in the footsteps of Luis Suarez as the only players to have won the Copa America while playing for Liverpool.

Alisson & Firmino's path to 2019 Copa America glory…

Group Phase
Bolivia – 3-0
Venezuela – 0-0
Peru – 5-0

Quarter-final
Paraguay – 0-0
(won 4-3 on pens)

Semi-final
Argentina – 2-0

Final
Peru – 3-1

CROSSWORD

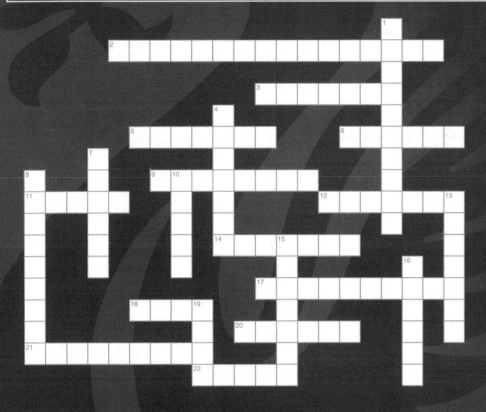

ACROSS

2 The club Jürgen Klopp managed prior to joining Liverpool.

3 Liverpool's training ground.

5 Area of Liverpool where Robbie Fowler is from.

6 The club Liverpool signed Alisson Becker from.

9 City in which Liverpool won the 2005 Champions League.

11 He came off the bench to score in the 2019 Champions League final.

12 Captained the 1984 treble winning team and later became manager.

14 Manager when Liverpool won the European Cup in 1977.

17 Dutch defender who Liverpool signed in July 2019.

18 Liverpool's record goalscorer.

20 The club Steven Gerrard joined after leaving Liverpool LA _____.

21 Full-back whose former clubs include Queens Park, Dundee United and Hull City.

22 Famous Liverpool supporter's song 'Poor Scouse _____'.

DOWN

1 Jordan Henderson's birthplace.

4 Liverpool's first European trophy.

7 Liverpool's official mascot _____ Red.

8 Number of goals Mo Salah scored for Liverpool in 2017/18.

10 Number of times Liverpool have won the FA Cup.

13 Sadio Mané's home country.

15 Name of the park that separates Anfield and Goodison.

16 Scottish team Virgil van Dijk once played for.

19 Liverpool's 1988 World Cup winner.

Answers on page 61.

ANOTHER SUPER NIGHT IN ISTANBUL

THE CITY OF ISTANBUL WILL ALWAYS HOLD A SPECIAL PLACE IN THE HEARTS OF EVERY LIVERPUDLIAN AND IN AUGUST 2019 IT WAS ONCE AGAIN THE SETTING FOR A MEMORABLE EUROPEAN TRIUMPH INVOLVING THE REDS.

14 August 2019
Besiktas Park, Istanbul

Liverpool: Adrian, Gomez, Robertson (Alexander-Arnold), Van Dijk, Matip, Fabinho, Milner (Wijnaldum), Henderson, Oxlaide-Chamberlain (Firmino), Mané (Origi), Salah.

Chelsea: Kepa, Azpilicueta, Christensen (Tomori), Zouma, Emerson, Kante, Jorginho, Kovacic (Barkley), Pedro, Giroud (Abraham), Pulisic (Mount).

Referee: Stephanie Frappart (France)

While the 2005 Champions League final could never be matched in terms of drama and importance, the 2019 UEFA Super Cup final further enhanced Liverpool's current status as Kings of Europe.

For the first time in history, this annual contest between the winners of the Champions League and Europa League featured two English clubs – adding extra spice to proceedings in Istanbul.

With Liverpool supporters far outnumbering those of Chelsea, Besiktas Park was a sea of red but it was the Blues who were celebrating first when Olivier Giroud opened the scoring in the 36th minute.

Sadio Mané equalised three minutes into the second-half, then added a second in extra-time only for Jorginho to level matters following the controversial award of a penalty just six minutes later.

By the time the final whistle eventually sounded on a hot and humid night the clock had ticked past midnight local time and a penalty shoot-out was required to determine who took the cup home.

Roberto Firmino, Fabinho, Divock Origi, Trent Alexander-Arnold and Mohamed Salah all stepped up to the spot and converted confidently for Liverpool, while Chelsea's first four takers did likewise.

That meant Tammy Abraham had to follow suit in order to force sudden death but Adrian, on his first full start for the club, denied him with an outstretched leg to seal a fourth UEFA Super Cup success for the club.

Significantly, it also took Liverpool's tally of 'elite' trophies won to 46, restoring its reputation as English football's most successful club.

ISTANBUL

TRENT ALEXANDER-ARNOLD

GEORGINIO WIJNALDUM

2019/20 SEASON TRACKER

KEEP YOUR OWN PERSONAL RECORD OF LIVERPOOL'S SEASON BY FILLING IN DETAILS OF ALL THE GAMES AS AND WHEN THEY ARE PLAYED…

Date	Opposition	Venue	Score	Scorers	Attendance
FA Community Shield					
4 Aug	Manchester City	Wembley			
UEFA Super Cup					
14 Aug	Chelsea	Istanbul			
FA Premier League					
9 Aug	Norwich City	H			
17 Aug	Southampton	A			
24 Aug	Arsenal	H			
31 Aug	Burnley	A			
14 Sep	Newcastle United	H			
22 Sep	Chelsea	A			
28 Sep	Sheffield United	A			
5 Oct	Leicester City	H			
20 Oct	Manchester United	A			
27 Oct	Tottenham Hotspur	H			
2 Nov	Aston Villa	A			
9 Nov	Manchester City	H			
23 Nov	Crystal Palace	A			
30 Nov	Brighton and Hove Albion	H			
4 Dec	Everton	H			
7 Dec	A.F.C. Bournemouth	A			
14 Dec	Watford	H			
21 Dec	West Ham United	A			
26 Dec	Leicester City	A			
28 Dec	Wolverhampton Wanderers	H			
2020					
1 Jan	Sheffield United	H			
11 Jan	Tottenham Hotspur	A			
18 Jan	Manchester United	H			
21 Jan	Wolverhampton Wanderers	A			
1 Feb	Southampton	H			
8 Feb	Norwich City	A			
22 Feb	West Ham United	H			

Date	Opposition	Venue	Score	Scorers	Attendance
29 Feb	Watford	A			
7 Mar	A.F.C. Bournemouth	H			
14 Mar	Everton	A			
21 Mar	Crystal Palace	H			
4 Apr	Manchester City	A			
11 Apr	Aston Villa	H			
18 Apr	Brighton and Hove Albion	A			
25 Apr	Burnley	H			
2 May	Arsenal	A			
9 May	Chelsea	H			
17 May	Newcastle United	A			

Please note: all fixtures correct at the time of going to print but are subject to potential change.

Date	Round	Opposition	Venue	Score	Scorers	Attendance
		Carabao Cup				
25 Sep	3rd round	MK Dons	A			
	4th round					
	Quarter-final					
	Semi-final 1st leg					
	Semi-final 2nd leg					
1 Mar	Final					
		Emirates FA Cup				
	3rd round					
	4th round					
	5th round					
	Quarter-final					
	Semi-final					
23 May	Final					
		Champions League				
17 Sep	Matchday One	Napoli	A			
2 Oct	Matchday Two	FC Salzburg	H			
23 Oct	Matchday Three	KRC Genk	A			
5 Nov	Matchday Four	KRC Genk	H			
27 Nov	Matchday Five	Napoli	H			
10 Dec	Matchday Six	FC Salzburg	A			
	Round of 16 1st leg					
	Round of 16 2nd leg					
	Quarter-final 1st leg					
	Quarter-final 2nd leg					
	Semi-final 1st leg					
	Semi-final 2nd leg					
30 May	Final					
		FIFA Club World Cup				
	Semi-final					
	Final or 3rd/4th play-off					

COMPETITION

To win a signed 2019/20 shirt answer this question:

How many times has Liverpool Football Club won the European Cup/ Champions League?

A: Five
B: Three
C: Six

Entry is by email only. Only one entry per contestant. Please enter LFC SHIRT followed by either A, B or C in the subject line of an email. In the body of the email, please include your full name, address, postcode, email address and phone number and send to: frontdesk@grangecommunications.co.uk by Friday 31st March 2020.

QUIZ AND PUZZLE ANSWERS

Page 24: Wordsearch

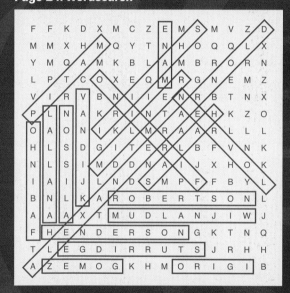

Page 53: Crossword

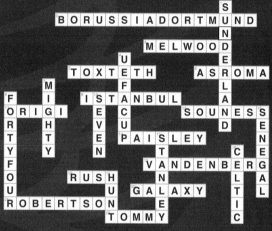

Page 41: When We Were Young

A. Henderson
Sunderland

B. Van Dijk
Groningen

C. Milner
Leeds

D. Wijnaldum
Feyenoord

WHERE'S MIGHTY RED?